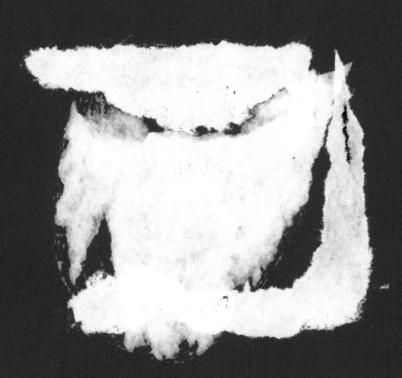

ELECTRICITY

Peter Riley

W
FRANKLIN WATTS
LONDON•SYDNEY

First published in 1998 by
Franklin Watts
96 Leonard Street, London
EC2A 4RH

Franklin Watts Australia
14 Mars Road
Lane Cove
NSW 2066

© Franklin Watts 1998
Text © Peter Riley 1998

Editor: Sarah Snashall
Art director: Robert Walster
Designer: Mo Choy
Picture research: Sue Mennell

Photography: Steve Shott
(unless otherwise credited)
Artwork: Sean Wilkinson

A CIP catalogue record for this
book is available from the
British Library.

ISBN 0 7496 2959 2

Dewey classification 537

Printed in Belgium

The publisher would like to
thank NES Arnold for the loan
of the electricity kit.

Picture credits:
Cover shot: Getty Images/
Richard Kavlin
Eye Ubiquitous/
Paul Thompson p.19 left
Getty Images title page and p.26
(Richard Kavlin), p.15 (Paul
Chesley)
Peter Hartley p.20
Image Bank/Grant V. Faint p.29 b
James Davis Travel
Photography p.19 right
Ray Muller p.23, p.28 top
NHPA/Dr Ivan Polunin p.27
Science Photo Library p.9
(US Department of Energy),
p.18 (Bruce Iverson)
Telegraph Colour Library/
Karin Slade p.5
Trip p.21 (N Ray), p.28 bottom
(H Rogers), p.29 (H Rogers)

CONTENTS

ELECTRICITY AROUND US

Electricity plays an important part in our lives. It can power an alarm clock to wake us up in the morning. It provides heat and light in our homes and powers television sets, CD players and computers. Some cars can even run on electricity.

A SIMPLE CIRCUIT

Electricity is a form of energy like heat and light. It moves along wires from an electrical supply to the object it is working. The movement of electricity is called the flow, or the current. In order for a current to flow, electricity has to move in a circular path called a circuit.

A simple circuit can be made from a cell or battery, some wire, a switch and a bulb. A cell is what we call a battery in everyday life. A battery is really a group of cells.

The battery is the store of electrical energy.

The bulb lights up when the switch is closed. This shows that electricity is moving around the circuit.

The wires let the electricity flow through them.

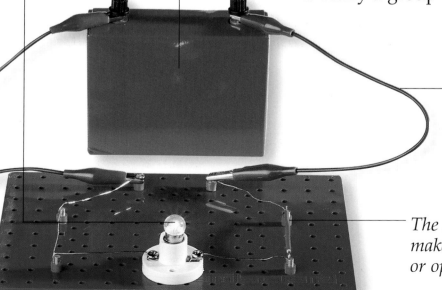

The switch can be closed to make the circuit complete, or opened to break it.

CIRCUITS EVERYWHERE

There are circuits in every piece of electrical equipment we use. A torch has a circuit with two cells, a light-bulb and a switch connected by metal strips.

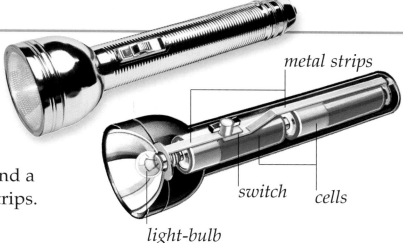

metal strips

switch

cells

light-bulb

These buildings have circuits on every floor. When they are switched on, electricity provides the power to light the rooms and work the equipment.

CLOSING THE GAPS

The wires are joined to terminals on the battery or cell. The places where the wires connect to the switch and the bulb are called the contacts. Electricity will only flow around the circuit if the wires are connected to the terminals and contacts and the switch is on. A gap anywhere in the circuit breaks it and stops the flow of electricity.

INVESTIGATE!

Take the cells out of a torch and look for the other parts of the circuit. Press the switch and see how it makes and breaks the circuit.

5

CELLS AND BATTERIES

In a simple circuit, the current of electricity is made in a cell or group of cells called a battery.

A CELL

A cell has a metal case and contains a paste. In the paste are chemicals. They make the current of electricity that flows around a circuit when the circuit is switched on.

The two places where wires are attached to the cell are called the terminals. One terminal is marked with a **+** sign. It is called the positive terminal. The other terminal is marked with a **–** sign. It is called the negative terminal. The current of electricity always flows around the circuit from the negative terminal to the positive terminal.

A BATTERY

A battery is a group of cells joined together. The positive terminal of one cell is joined to the negative terminal of the cell next to it. The cells are placed next to each other in a box. The positive and negative terminals of the battery stick out of the top of the box.

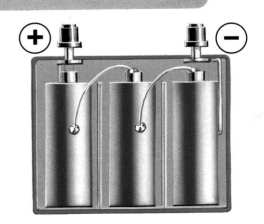

In this potato clock, each potato works as a cell. The metal sticking into the potato and the chemicals in the potato make electricity.

VOLTAGE

The power of a cell or battery to make an electric current is measured in volts. The number of volts is called the voltage. The voltage of a cell is marked on its case. There is a number followed by the letter V. A cell with 1.5 V marked on its side has a voltage of 1.5 volts.

When cells are joined together to make a battery the power of the battery is the power of each cell added together. If there are three 1.5 V cells in a battery the voltage of the battery is 1.5 + 1.5 + 1.5 = 4.5 V.

INVESTIGATE!

Find some items in your home that run on cells. Count the number of cells each needs to run. Work out the voltage that each item needs.

CONDUCTORS AND INSULATORS

Electricity can travel around a circuit because the wire in the circuit allows the electricity to flow through it. The wire is a conductor of electricity. Electricity does not pass through all materials. Materials that do not conduct electricity are called electrical insulators.

TESTING MATERIALS

A simple way to sort materials into conductors and insulators is to set up a circuit with a gap in it. The material to be tested is placed across the gap. If the material is a conductor, electricity flows around the circuit and makes the bulb light up. If the material is an insulator, electricity does not flow and the bulb does not light up.

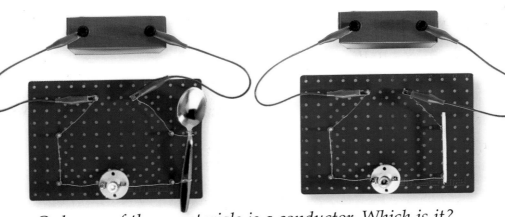

Only one of these materials is a conductor. Which is it?

CONDUCTORS

Any metal material tested in the circuit will make the bulb light because all metals are conductors. One substance that is not a metal but conducts electricity is graphite. Graphite is the black substance that is used to make the lead in a pencil. Water is also a conductor of electricity.

INSULATORS

Most materials do not conduct electricity. Clothing materials such as wool and cotton are insulators. Building materials such as stone, brick, wood, glass and plastic are also insulators.

These pottery discs are insulators and are used to hold power cables safely on electricity pylons.

KEEPING SAFE

Electricity is dangerous and should not be touched. Care must be taken when handling any electrical equipment. You can keep safe by only touching the plastic parts of an electrical object and by drying your hands before touching light switches.

An electricity sign warns you away from high levels of electricity.

Electricity is conducted to equipment through a metal lead and plug. The lead and plug are covered in plastic to stop the electricity from reaching your hand.

▮ INVESTIGATE!

Set up the circuit shown on page 8. Test some metal, graphite, wood and plastic to see which ones light the light-bulb.

SWITCHES

The flow of electricity in a circuit is controlled by a switch. It either lets electricity flow around the circuit or it stops it from flowing.

ON AND OFF

A switch is a piece of metal that can be moved. One end of the metal is connected to a wire in the circuit. The other end can be moved to touch a contact in the circuit. When the end is touching the contact the switch is 'on'.

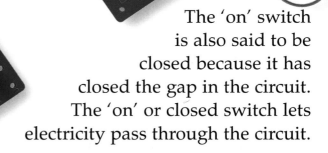

The 'on' switch is also said to be closed because it has closed the gap in the circuit. The 'on' or closed switch lets electricity pass through the circuit.

The switch is 'off' or open when the end of the metal is not touching the contact. A gap is made in the circuit. Electricity cannot pass through the gap, so electricity cannot pass around the circuit.

THE LIGHT SWITCH ON THE WALL

Inside the light switch on the wall are two pieces of metal. When you press the switch, a piece of plastic pushes on one of the pieces of metal and moves it. When the light is switched on, the metal is moved to touch the other piece of metal. The electricity can now flow through the circuit and the light comes on.

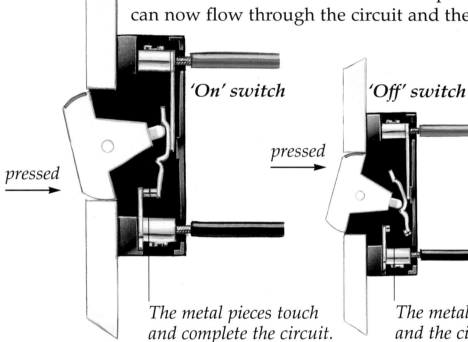

'On' switch

pressed

pressed

'Off' switch

When the light is switched off, the metal in the switch is moved away from the other piece of metal. The electricity stops flowing and the light goes out.

The metal pieces touch and complete the circuit.

The metal pieces do not touch and the circuit is broken.

INVESTIGATE!

Use a simple circuit to flash a message using this code (called Morse Code). A dot is a short flash and a dash is a long flash.

A • –	J • – – –	S • • •	2 • • – – –
B – • • •	K – • –	T –	3 • • • – –
C – • – •	L • – • •	U • • –	4 • • • • –
D – • •	M – –	V • • • –	5 • • • • •
E •	N – •	W • – –	6 – • • • •
F • • – •	O – – –	X – • • –	7 – – • • •
G – – •	P • – – •	Y – • – –	8 – – – • •
H • • • •	Q – – • –	Z – – • •	9 – – – – •
I • •	R • – •	1 • – – – –	0 – – – – –

11

HEAT AND LIGHT

The metal in a wire pushes against the flow of electricity passing through it. This push is called the resistance. The current of electricity has to push harder than the resistance to get through the wire. If the resistance of the wire is very strong (or 'high') the electricity may make the wire hot as it pushes through it.

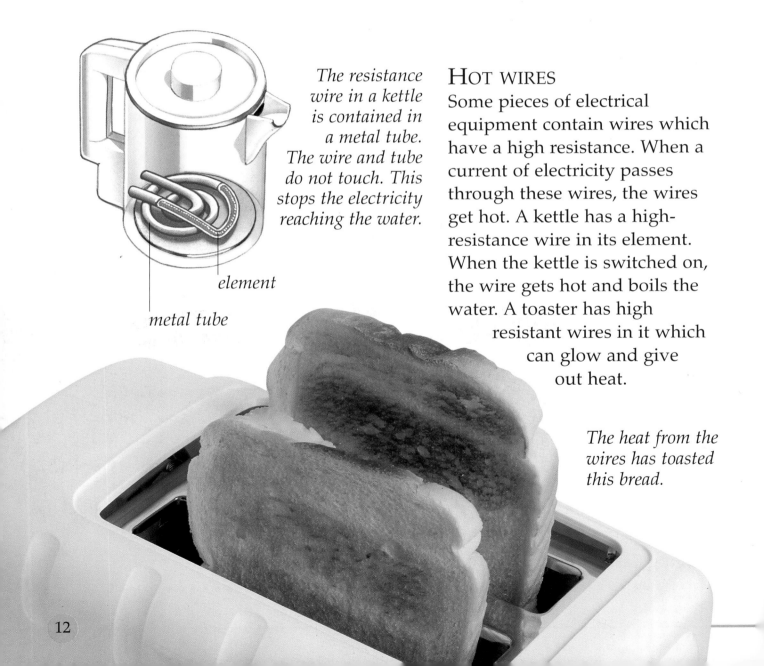

The resistance wire in a kettle is contained in a metal tube. The wire and tube do not touch. This stops the electricity reaching the water.

element

metal tube

HOT WIRES
Some pieces of electrical equipment contain wires which have a high resistance. When a current of electricity passes through these wires, the wires get hot. A kettle has a high-resistance wire in its element. When the kettle is switched on, the wire gets hot and boils the water. A toaster has high resistant wires in it which can glow and give out heat.

The heat from the wires has toasted this bread.

FUSES

If a fault develops in a piece of electrical equipment, a large current may flow through it. The equipment may get so hot that it catches fire. A fuse is fitted to the equipment to stop a large current flowing.

The fuse contains a wire which melts and breaks if the current gets too large. We say the fuse 'blows'. The broken wire stops the current like an open switch and the equipment does not get hot and catch fire.

IN A LIGHT-BULB

The wire in a light-bulb is called the filament. It is made of the metal tungsten. Its resistance is so high that when a current of electricity flows through it, the wire gets so hot that it glows and gives out light.

When the current of electricity has passed through the filament for a long time, the metal becomes weak and eventually snaps. When this happens, the current can no longer flow and the bulb does not light up. It is time for a new light-bulb.

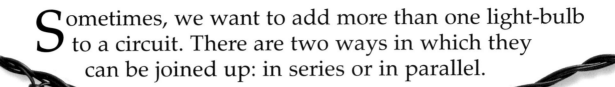

LIGHT-BULBS IN CIRCUITS

Sometimes, we want to add more than one light-bulb to a circuit. There are two ways in which they can be joined up: in series or in parallel.

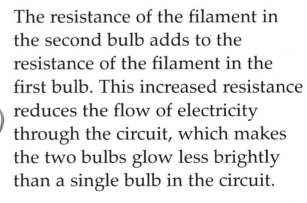

Fairy lights are often wired in series. If one bulb fails, they all go out. Testing to find the broken bulb may take a long time.

BULBS IN SERIES

The simplest way to add a second bulb to a circuit is to put it in line with the first. Only one wire is needed to join the two bulbs together. Bulbs that are joined together in a line are said to be arranged in series.

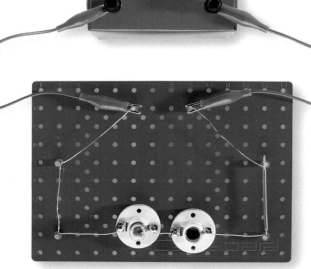

The resistance of the filament in the second bulb adds to the resistance of the filament in the first bulb. This increased resistance reduces the flow of electricity through the circuit, which makes the two bulbs glow less brightly than a single bulb in the circuit.

These bulbs are in series. If one of the bulbs fails, or is removed, the circuit is broken and the other bulb goes out.

ADDING BULBS IN PARALLEL

A bulb can also be added to a circuit in parallel. To do this, a new circuit is created for the new bulb. When the current is switched on it flows through each bulb separately.

The resistance of the filament in the second bulb does not add to the resistance of the filament in the first bulb. More current passes through bulbs in parallel than through bulbs in series. Bulbs in parallel glow more brightly.

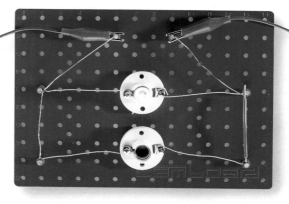

These bulbs are in parallel. If one of the bulbs fails, or is removed, the other bulb does not go out because it is still in a circuit with the battery.

Bulbs in homes and streets are connected in parallel so that if one bulb fails all the other bulbs stay on.

■ INVESTIGATE!

Set up a circuit like the one on page 14. Add a third bulb. What happens to the brightness of the bulbs?

CONTROLLING THE FLOW

Sometimes we need to increase or decrease the flow of electricity in a circuit. This can be done by changing the number of batteries or bulbs. The brightness of the bulbs shows how the current changes when batteries or bulbs are added or taken away from the circuit.

ADDING BULBS

The flow of current can be reduced by increasing the resistance in a circuit. When bulbs are added in series, the resistance in the circuit is increased and the flow of electricity is reduced.

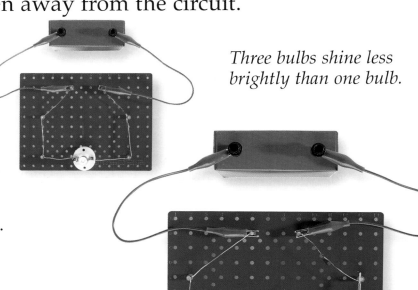

Three bulbs shine less brightly than one bulb.

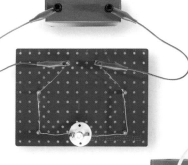

The extra battery makes the bulb shine more brightly.

ADDING BATTERIES

A battery contains the force to push a current of electricity around a circuit. When two batteries are joined in series they provide twice the push of one battery on its own and make a stronger current.

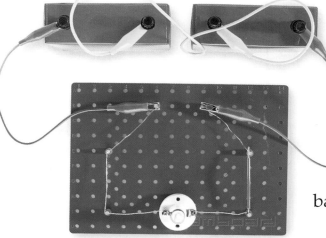

VARYING THE RESISTANCE

The flow of electricity can also be changed by using a variable resistor. A variable resistor changes the resistance in a circuit, and this changes the current. The volume control on a radio is a variable resistor. As you turn it, you change the amount of electricity flowing to the loudspeaker.

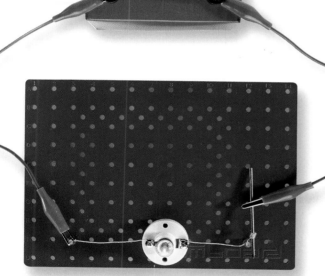

MAKING A VARIABLE RESISTOR

In this circuit, a variable resistor has been made by connecting graphite from a pencil into the circuit. Graphite has a higher resistance than the wire in the circuit.

One of the contacts touching the graphite can be moved to change the length of graphite in the circuit. This changes the resistance in the circuit.

When a long length of graphite is used, the resistance in the circuit is high and the bulb shines faintly. What will happen if a shorter length of graphite is used?

■ INVESTIGATE!

Ask an adult to help you open up a pencil to remove the graphite. Set up the circuit on this page. Can you make the bulb shine brightly? Can you make the bulb go out?

THE ELECTRIC MOTOR

When electricity flows through a coil of wire, it makes the coil behave like a magnet. If a wire coil with a current going through it is put between a pair of magnets, the coil spins. The spinning coil can be used to make an electric motor.

THE POLES OF A MAGNET

Magnets have two places where their magnetic force is strongest. These places are called the north pole and the south pole.

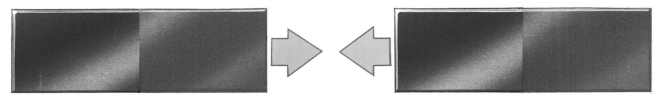

If a north pole and a south pole are brought together and released, their forces pull them together.

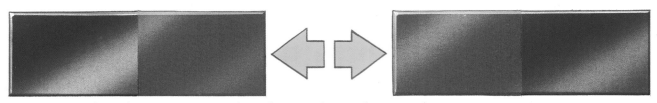

If two north poles or two south poles are brought together and released, their forces push each other away.

Inside an electric motor.

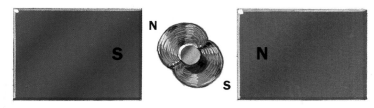

HOW THE MOTOR WORKS

Inside an electric motor there is a coil of wire with a current running through it. The current of electricity gives the coil of wire a north pole and a south pole. The coil is placed between two magnets.

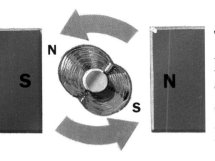

The north pole of the coil is attracted to the south pole of the magnet, and the south pole of the coil is attracted to the north pole of the magnet. These forces of attraction turn the coil around so that the south pole of the magnet faces the north pole of the coil.

The contacts in the coil are set up so that at this point the current changes direction and flows around the coil in the opposite direction. The part of the coil facing the north pole of the magnet now also has a north pole. The coil is repelled by the magnet and spins around again.

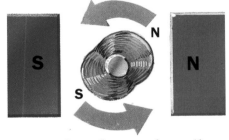

The current continues to change direction, and this makes the coil spin around and around. If the coil is connected to a wheel through a motor shaft, the wheel spins around as the coil spins.

The magnetic poles on the coil are changed to keep the coil spinning.

ELECTRIC MOTORS EVERYWHERE

Small electric motors are used to turn CDs and tape cassettes. Large electric motors drive washing machines and power drills. A huge electric motor is used to pull a train.

An electric motor turns the wheels on an electric train.

Electric motors can be used to make electric cars.

GENERATING ELECTRICITY

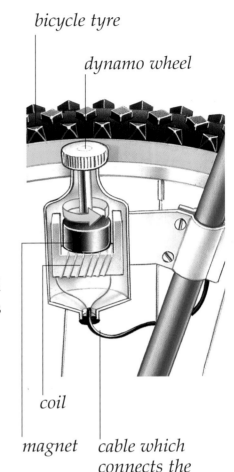

bicycle tyre

dynamo wheel

coil

magnet   cable which
connects the
coil to the lamp

As we have seen, if a coil with a current passing through it is put between two magnets, it can be made to spin. In a similar way, if a spinning magnet is put near a wire coil, an electric current will be generated in the coil.

THE DYNAMO

A dynamo is used to generate electricity to light the lamp on a bicycle. It has a wheel at the top which touches the tyre wall. As the bicycle wheel turns, the tyre wall rushes past the dynamo wheel and makes it spin. Inside the dynamo the wheel is attached to a magnet. As the dynamo wheel spins the magnet inside the dynamo spins too. There is a wire coil near the magnet. When the magnet spins it produces an electric current in the wire coil. The current passes along wires connected to the bicycle frame and lights the lamp.

Electricity provides light for the cyclist to see the road in the dark.

▌INVESTIGATE!

See how the amount of light changes in a bicycle bulb when you spin the dynamo wheel slowly then fast.

Inside a power station.

THE ELECTRIC GENERATOR

Most of the electricity we use is generated in power stations. An electric generator at a power station is like a gigantic dynamo. Around the generator walls are huge coils of wire and down its centre is a magnet shaped like a cylinder. The magnet is attached to a shaft which passes out of the generator.

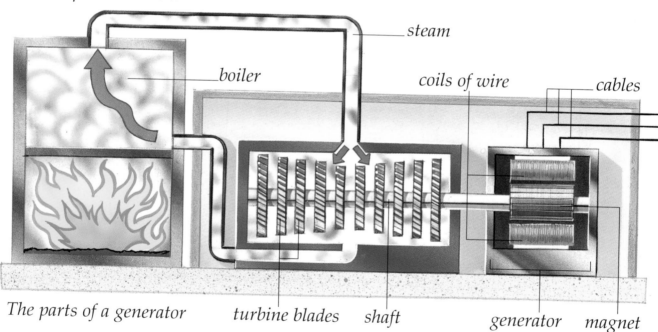

The parts of a generator   *turbine blades*   *shaft*   *generator*   *magnet*

steam

boiler

coils of wire

cables

In most kinds of power stations, the generator shaft is attached to turbine blades. Water is heated in a boiler to make fast moving steam which is directed over the blades and makes them turn and spin the shaft. The shaft spins the magnet in the generator. The spinning magnet generates a current of electricity in the wires. The current is passed along cables in the air or underground to towns and cities far away.

ELECTRICITY IN YOUR HOME

Electricity reaches your home through a cable which is connnected to a power station which may be many kilometres away. When electricity enters your home it takes many different paths through your home and is used in a variety of ways.

Electricity first passes through a meter which records how much electricity is used, then moves into consumer unit. This contains fuses or devices to break circuits if the current in them gets too large. Electricity can flow from the consumer unit to any of the circuits in the house which are switched on.

The electric cooker has its own circuit because it uses a large current.

There is a ceiling light circuit on each floor. The circuits are opened and closed by switches on the walls.

There is a ring main on each floor. It has sockets in the wall which many different kinds of electrical device can be plugged into.

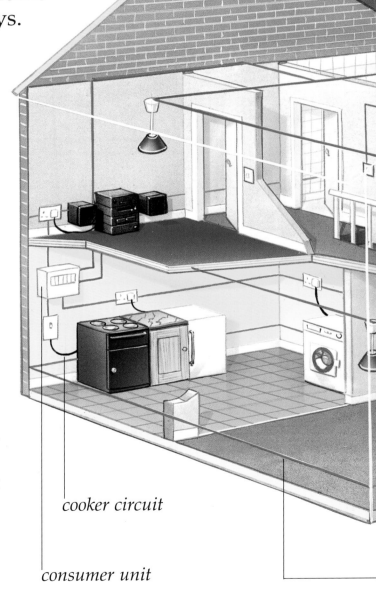

cooker circuit

consumer unit

ceiling light circuit

ringmain

USES OF ELECTRICITY

Electricity in a house provides heat for boiling a kettle, warming bath water, cooking food, heating rooms through electric fires and radiators.

Light shines from light-bulbs and tubes, and glows from liquid-crystal displays as electricity passes through them.

Electric motors spin compact discs and turn audio and video tapes, microwave ovens, turn-tables, washing machines and dryers, food mixers and power drills.

Electricity flows through aerials and satellite dishes to pick up signals that make radios and televisions work. It gives power to a computer and through a telephone line links it to the Internet.

■ INVESTIGATE!

How many different ways is electricity used in your home?

STATIC ELECTRICITY

E very substance is made of tiny particles called atoms. Inside each atom are even smaller particles called electrons. When certain substances are rubbed together, the electrons move from one substance to the other. This gives both substances an electric charge which does not move called static electricity.

MAKING STATIC ELECTRICITY

There are two kinds of electric charge. They are called positive charge and negative charge. An electron has a negative charge.

If a balloon is rubbed on a woollen jumper, some electrons leave the jumper and collect on the balloon. The extra electrons on the balloon give it a negative electric charge. The lack of electrons on the jumper give it a positive charge.

The two different charges attract each other. When the balloon is pressed onto the jumper, it stays in place because the negative charge on the balloon attracts the positive charge on the jumper. The two charged objects are pulled together.

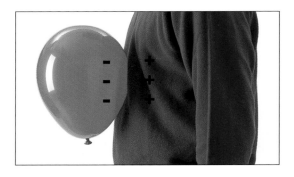

ONE CHARGE MAKING ANOTHER

A charged object can drive away electrons from the surface of another object, or it can draw more electrons to its surface. When this happens the surface of the second object also becomes charged.

A plastic pen becomes negatively charged when it is rubbed with a cloth. If it is placed near a small scrap of paper the negative charge makes one surface of the scrap of paper positive. The strength of attraction between the two charges makes the paper scrap spring up to the pen and stick to it.

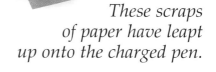

These scraps of paper have leapt up onto the charged pen.

■ INVESTIGATE!

Rub some polystyrene with a woollen cloth. Hold the polystyrene over a friend's hair. The hair will rise because of the charge the polystyrene makes on the hair. The strands of hair will separate because they all have the same charge and repel each other.

The charged hair stands on end.

⚡ ELECTRICITY IN NATURE

Electricity is not just made in batteries and power stations, it also can be found in nature. It is generated in storm clouds and in the bodies of animals.

LIGHTNING

Lightning is made when a very large charge of static electricity builds up in a storm cloud. The static electricity is made by the winds inside the clouds rubbing ice particles together.

The top of the cloud becomes positively charged and the bottom of the cloud becomes negatively charged.

When the charges get very high, the air between them can no longer act as an insulator and a huge current of electricity flows. This makes a flash of light inside the cloud called sheet lightning.

The negative charge at the base of a storm cloud drives away negative charge from the surface of the ground and makes it positively charged. The difference in charge between the cloud and the ground may become so high that lightning flashes between them. This is called forked lightning.

When lightning flashes it destroys all the charges.

ELECTRIC FISH

The electric eel of South American rivers, the electric catfish of African rivers and the electric ray which is found in most seas all have parts of their bodies which can make large amounts of electricity. They use this electricity to catch fish by releasing electricity into the water around them. The electricity does not harm the electric fish, but it kills or stuns any fish nearby. The dead or stunned fish are then easy to catch and eat.

ELECTRICITY IN THE BODY

The brain and nerves of humans and animals make electric currents which flow through them. The electric currents control the activity of the body and keep it alive.

INVESTIGATE!

Find out how fast messages travel from your eye to your hand muscles by asking a friend to drop a ruler between your finger and thumb and seeing how fast you can catch it.

ELECTRONIC MESSAGES

There are many different devices that can be put into a circuit. They are called electronic components and they can change the size and direction of the current in the circuit. These changes can be used to send messages around the world.

The microphone and loudspeaker are connected to wires which link into a circuit with another telephone.

THE TELEPHONE

A current of electricity flows through the wires that connect telephones. A telephone handset has a microphone in the mouthpiece and a loudspeaker in the earpiece. When you speak into the microphone, the resistance of the microphone changes with every word and sends currents of different strengths to the loudspeaker in the telephone of the listener. The electrical energy in the currents is turned into sound energy in the loudspeaker and the listener hears your words.

A computer can be connected into a telephone circuit which forms part of a network called the Internet. It allows people to send messages between their computers.

RADIO WAVES

When an electric current in a circuit is made to travel one way and then the other many times in a second, it makes radio waves that travel through the air. Electronic components in the circuit can change the size and speed of the waves and messages can be sent out as a pattern of changing waves. The radio waves are sent out from a transmitter, across the country or across the world.

Mobile phones have a transmitter and a receiver so that messages can be carried by radio waves instead of wires.

A satellite dish directs radio waves to the receiver at its centre so that the messages they carry can be converted into currents of electricity.

The messages in the radio waves are detected by a receiver. This has a circuit with electronic components that change the message carried by the waves into electrical currents which can be used to work a loudspeaker, a television or computer screen or a fax machine.

GLOSSARY

AERIAL – a metal rod which collects radio waves on a radio or television set.

ATOM – a tiny particle which is made of even smaller particles. At its centre is a nucleus made from particles called protons and neutrons. Moving around the nucleus are smaller particles still. They are called electrons.

BATTERY – a group of cells joined together. The battery may be made of cylindrical cells (like those used in a torch) joined together by wires as part of an investigation or it may may be made in a factory where the cells are stacked in a box.

CELL – a metal container which holds chemicals that can make electricity flow in a circuit. In everyday life we call a cell a battery.

CD – A compact disc on which music is recorded. CDs can also be used to store information for computers.

CIRCUIT – a path along which a current of electricity can be made to pass. It has a source of electricity, such as a cell, wires and a switch. It can also include other electrical devices such as a motor or a buzzer.

CONTACT – a piece of metal that connects a wire to a device in a circuit.

CURRENT – the flow of electricity in a circuit.

DYNAMO – a device which contains a magnet and a wire coil and is used on a bicycle to generate electricity for the lights as the bicycle moves along.

EEL – a type of fish with a long cylindrical body. Most kinds of eel do not generate electricity.

ELECTRICAL CONDUCTOR – a material such as a metal that a current of electricity can pass through.

ELECTRICAL INSULATOR – a material such as pottery that a current of electricity cannot pass through.

ELECTRON – a very small particle in an atom which has a negative electrical charge. Electrons can be moved between some materials by rubbing the materials together.

ELEMENT – a wire with a high resistance which produces heat when the circuit is switched on.

FILAMENT – a coiled thread of wire in a light-bulb through which electricity passes. When this happens the metal in the filament becomes so hot it gives out light.

FUSE – a device which contains a wire that melts and breaks a circuit if the current in it becomes too high and could start a fire. Fuses are used in circuits in the home and in plugs.

GENERATOR – a machine at a power station which contains a magnet surrounded by coils of wire. The magnet is connected to a rod called a shaft. When the shaft is made to spin, the magnet spins. The spinning magnet generates electricity in the coils of wire.

GRAPHITE – a black substance made from carbon which conducts electricity like a metal. It is used to make the lead in a pencil.

LEAD – a plastic coated wire for carrying electricity from the mains to an electrical device such as a computer.

LIQUID-CRYSTAL DISPLAY – an arrangement of liquid crystals and electrical circuits used in some clocks and calculators to display numbers.

LOUDSPEAKER – an electrical device which converts the flow of an electric current into sound waves.

MICROPHONE – an electrical device which converts sound waves into an electrical current.

MORSE CODE – a code of dots and dashes invented by Samuel Morse in 1837 to send messages by electrical currents on long wires called telegraph wires.

MOTOR SHAFT – a rod connected to the wire coil in a motor. It is also connected to a wheel that is used to provide movement, such as to turn tapes, CDs or parts of a washing machine. The wire coil makes the shaft turn and the shaft makes the wheel turn.

NERVE – a long fibre which carries electrical messages inside the body. Nerves are found in all kinds of animals.

PLUG – an electrical device with one or more metal pins surrounded by insulating material for connecting a lead into mains electricity or a wire into a circuit.

POLYSTYRENE – a type of solid foam. It is good for making static electricity.

SWITCH – a device in a circuit which is used to make the electricity flow around the circuit or to stop it from flowing.

TERMINAL – a place where a wire is connected to a cell or a battery.

TUNGSTEN – a metal used to make the filaments in light-bulbs.

TURBINE BLADES – long, flat pieces of metal arranged on a shaft connected to a magnet in a power station generator. Fast-moving steam pushes on them to spin the shaft and the magnet so that electricity can be made.

VARIABLE RESISTOR – a device with a movable contact which is used to change the level of resistance in a circuit. The greater the resistance in the circuit, the smaller the current will be.

VOLTAGE – a measure of the electrical energy in a cell or battery. The voltage is written on the side of the cell or battery as a number with the letter V after it.

INDEX